And now introduce yourself. . . .

Name: _____

Address: _____

Phone Number: _____

School: _____

Teacher: _____

Principal: _____

Knock-Knock

Knock-knock. *Who's there?*
Stink. *Stink who?*
Stink you'd know
your own little brother.

Knock-knock. *Who's there?*
Frank. *Frank who?*
Frank you for the
birthday present.

Knock-knock. *Who's there?*
Toad. *Toad who?*
Toad you to keep out
of my room!

Knock-knock. *Who's there?*
Hedda. *Hedda who?*
Hedda toad named
Toady, but I let him go.

Judy Moody's

Double-Rare Way-Not-Boring Book of Fun Stuff to Do

Megan McDonald   illustrated by Peter H. Reynolds

CANDLEWICK PRESS

Meet Judy Moody!

Name: Judy Moody

Address: 117 Croaker Road

Phone Number: 555-JUDY

School: Virginia Dare School

Teacher: Mr. Todd

Principal: Ms. Tuxedo

Jokes!!

Knock-knock. *Who's there?*
Newt. *Newt who?*
Newt England is where the American Revolution started.

Knock-knock. *Who's there?*
Pasture. *Pasture who?*
Pasture bedtime, Stink!

Knock-knock. *Who's there?*
Pencil. *Pencil who?*
Pencil-vania.

Now it's your turn! Can you write some jokes that will *knock-knock* your socks off?

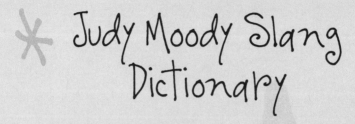

Judy Moody Slang Dictionary

From *double rare* to *star-spangled bananas*, here's a look at some of Judy Moody's favorite expressions. With this Judy Moody slang dictionary, you'll never be at a loss for words — and that's definitely double cool!

rare!: cool!

double rare!: way cool!

double cool!: twice as cool!

ROAR!: what to say when you're angry or frustrated

pizza table: the little plastic piece that keeps a pizza from touching the top of the pizza box

bothers: little brothers who bother you all the time!

smad: sad and mad, at the same time!

same-same: what you say when you and your friend do something that's the same

phoney baloney: fake

not-boring: interesting

boing!: aha!

star-spangled bananas!: what you say when you're surprised or amazed

L.B.S.: Long Boring Story

Ouch Face: the face you make when someone's pulling your hair

ABC gum: Already Been Chewed gum

nark: bad mood

T. P. Club: the Toad Pee Club

oogley: gross

caterpillar eyebrow: the way your eyebrows look when you're in a mood (not a good mood, a bad mood!)

or something: what you say when someone presents you with a list of choices that end with "or something" and you don't agree with any of the choices

V.I.Q.: Very Important Question

Antarctica: the desk at the back of Mr. Todd's classroom where you have to sit if you're causing trouble

goopy: cheesy

Who's Who

Who's who in the Judy Moody world? Fill in the speech bubbles to show what you think Judy and her friends are saying. Use the slang dictionary to help you!

Judy

Queen of moods

Mom

Judy's mother

Stink

Judy's little *bother*

Dad

Judy's father

Who's Who in Your Life?

Draw or paste pictures of your family, friends, and pets in the circles below, and write your own mini-descriptions of each person below their picture. Don't forget to include yourself!

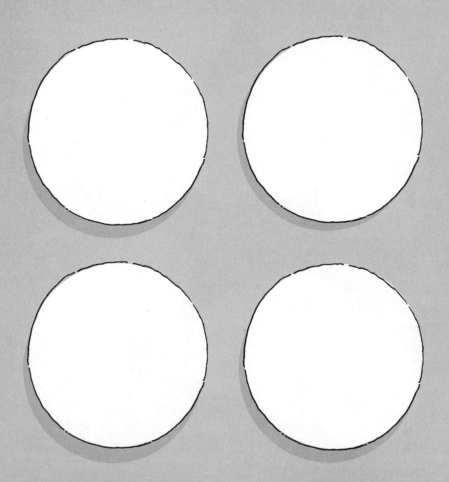

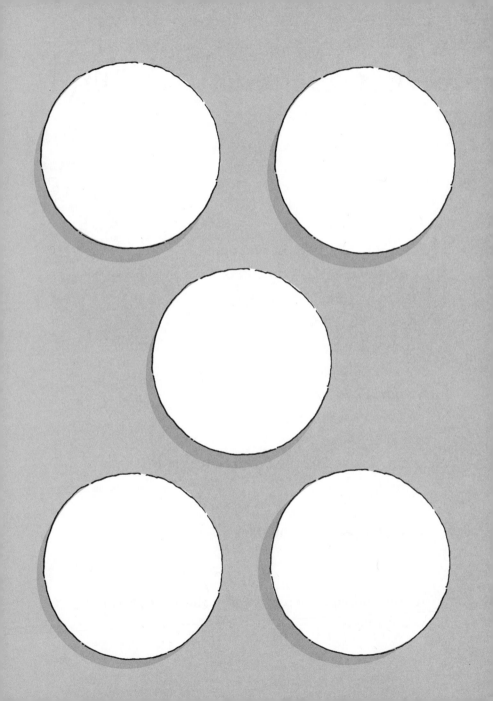

Be a Screamin' Mimi!

I scream
You scream
We all scream
FOR ICE CREAM!

Screamin' Mimi's is the real name
of an ice-cream shop in author
Megan McDonald's hometown of
Sebastopol, California. Megan's
favorite flavor is coffee ice cream
with chocolate chips. Judy Moody's
favorite flavors are Chocolate Mud
and Rain Forest Mist.

What is your favorite flavor of ice cream?

What toppings do you like?

**If you had your own ice-cream shop, what would
you name it?**

Did you know...

The idea for *Judy Moody Gets Famous!* came to Megan McDonald when she was at Screamin' Mimi's. She didn't want to forget her idea, so she wrote it down on a Screamin' Mimi's napkin!

Try it! Get a plain paper napkin and list some of YOUR ideas to write about.

Use the drawing at right to build your own ice-cream cone. Color it in to make it look "scooper" delicious. Use your favorite flavors as inspiration!

Top flavor: _____

Middle flavor: _____

Bottom flavor: _____

Here's a poem all about Judy Moody, and it spells her name. It's called an acrostic.

Jaws is her favorite pet.

Under her pillow is the dictionary.

Declares independence from brushing her hair.

Yuck! Member of the Toad Pee Club!

Moods, good and bad.

Or something!

Operates on a zucchini.

Dresses up as Elizabeth Blackwell, First Woman Doctor.

Yes, she really did eat a shark.

Spell YOUR name in an acrostic below,
and make up a poem all about YOU!

_____ _____

_____ _____

_____ _____

_____ _____

_____ _____

_____ _____

_____ _____

_____ _____

Collections

Judy and her friends love to collect things!

Judy collects:

pizza tables
scabs
toothpicks
Band-Aids
spare doll parts
baseball erasers

Frank collects:

marbles
rubber bugs
erasers
buffalo nickels
comic books
miniature soaps

How many items are in your best collection?

What's the most unusual collection you have?

Try starting a collection that's RARE. Some ideas are:
books with mistakes, old stamps, old buttons, fossils,
autographs, four-leaf clovers, coins that aren't round. . . .

Furry Friends

Here's a list of Judy's stuffed animals:

Ned Bear
Ted Bear
Fred Bear
Cornflake (not-cloned Guineapig)
Brownie
Tookie (Toucan)
Snowflake (Loon from Minnesota)
Auggie
Doggie
Pepper (smells like pepper)

What stuffed animals do you have?

Are there any that have a special meaning?

Any you've had since you
were a baby?

My Room

Judy's favorite spot to hang out is her top bunk. What's your favorite place to read, think, dream?

Here's what you might find under Judy Moody's bed:

- ☺ pizza tables
- ☺ a dried-up prune
- ☺ Mouse
- ☺ dust bunnies
- ☺ a lost sock

What's lurking in the dust under your bed?

Are you neat or messy?

Where do you fit on the scale below?

___ Neat freak

___ Slightly disheveled

___ Neat enough

~ cHAos!

In a messy mood? Clean it up!

- Hang up a bulletin board where you can collect your notes, postcards, ticket stubs, and other stuff you want to save.

- Give away something you don't need anymore to a friend.

- Pick up ten things from the floor.

- Decorate boxes to keep your stuff in.

In a party mood?

- Put up a string of fun lights, like chili peppers or sunflowers.

- Put your birthday cards on a string and hang it on the wall.

- Get a Mylar balloon and let it float to the ceiling.

- Hang paper streamers or a paper chain from the ceiling or around your bed.

In a nature mood?

- Collect some rocks, shells, or colored beach glass, leaves, acorns, or pinecones to display on your bookcase or windowsill.

- Decorate your window with paper snowflakes.

- Hang a crystal in your window and watch it make rainbows on the walls.

- Be a stargazer — stick glow-in-the-dark stars and planets to your ceiling.

Trace and cut out the doorknob hanger below to keep your "bothers" and sisters out of your room!

You can write your own message on the other side — be creative!

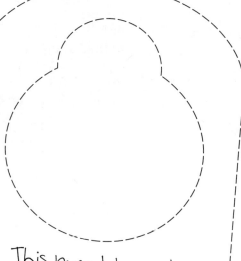

This room belongs to

_____

KEEP OUT!

(This means you,_____.)

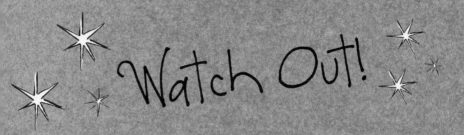

Watch Out!

If you get too close to a volcano, you might catch:

PNEUMONOULTRAMICROSCOPICSILICOVOLCANOCONIOSIS
from breathing the volcano dust!

Wow! The longest word in the dictionary — not
even Jessica Finch, Queen Bee, can spell that!

How many words can you make using only
those 45 letters? A couple are listed below
to get you started:

cranium

ultramarine

_____

_____

_____

_____

_____

_____

_____

_____

_____

_____

Now try doing the same with
ANTIDISESTABLISHMENTARIANISM
or with
HIPPOPOTOMONSTROSESQUIPEDALIAN.
(Find out what these words mean at the back of the book.)

Make a ME Collage!

You can draw or cut out pictures and paste things to your collage. Here are some ideas to get you started:

- Who I am
- Where I live
- My friends
- My best friend
- My favorite pet
- When I grow up . . .
- Hobbies

- Clubs
- The best thing that ever happened to me
- The worst thing that ever happened to me
- The funniest thing that ever happened to me

Write down your ideas here, but make your final
collage on a separate piece of paper or poster board.
Be creative! It's all about what makes you YOU.

_____

_____

_____

_____

_____

_____

Judy Moody

and her friends are part of a very special club: the T. P. Club.

Do you belong to any clubs?

Did you know that all of the clubs below are real?

- National Rhyming Names Club
- Left-Handers Club
- Rubber Ducky Fan Club
- Bubblegum Club

Invent your own club! What should it be called?

Don't forget to go to www.judymoody.com
to join the Official Judy Moody Fan Club!

Record-Breaking Ideas

The members of the T. P. Club tried to break the world record for the longest human centipede. Here are some other crazy records — for real!

- If you're older than 6, it's too late to be the youngest world line-dance champion, but you still have time to become the youngest doctor (17 years old)!

- If you can get more than 72,000 people together, you can do the world's largest chicken dance!

- You can always just grow your toenails . . . but each one would have to be almost 9 inches long! Ewwww!

What record would you really like to break?

Can you think of a new record you'd like to set?

Judy Moody Gets Famous!

She, Judy Moody, Phantom Doll Doctor, now felt as famous as Queen Elizabeth, as famous as George Washington, as famous as Superman. **FAMOUSER!**

Excerpt from *Judy Moody Gets Famous!*

Judy Moody finally gets her chance to be famous. What about you?

What would you like to be famous for? Draw or paste your picture on the front page of the newspaper on the next page and write your own headline above it. Now you can be in your family's **HALL OF FAME** — just like Judy!

All About Pets

Give your pet a makeover!

Before

After

Draw or paste a picture of your pet below.
Now draw a funny outfit on him or her!

Do you have any pets?

If so, which is your favorite?

If not, what pet would you like to have?

What's your pet's greatest talent?
Add your pets to the chart below:

Judy

pet: Mouse

species: cat

talent: makes toast!

pet: Jaws

species: Venus flytrap

talent: eats hamburger

Stink

pet: Toady

species: toad

talent: initiates members
of the T. P. Club

Frank

pet: Sparky

species: dog

talent: jumps through
a Hula-Hoop

Rocky

pet: Houdini

species: iguana

talent: can lose his tail

Your pets

pet:

species:

talent:

pet:

species:

talent:

pet:

species:

talent:

Make a Difference!
Heal the World!

"I'm going to live
up here now. Like Julia
Butterfly Hill."

"Who?"

"The girl who lived in
a tree for two years. Mr.
Todd told us. They were
going to cut down some
ancient redwoods in California, so Julia Butterfly
Hill climbed one of the trees and stayed there.
They couldn't cut down a tree with a person in it.
She even named the tree Luna."

"You can't just live in a tree, Judy," said Stink.

"Judy Monarch Moody to you."

Excerpt from *Judy Moody Saves the World!*

Save the Rain Forest!
Save the Animals! World Peace!
What will you do to change YOUR world?
How will YOU make a difference?

Choose one idea and do something about it.
Here are some ways to get started:

Make a sign.

Write a letter.

Start a petition. Get your
friends to sign it.

Put on a play to raise
awareness.

Have a sale to raise
money for your cause.

_____

_____

_____

_____

_____

ENDANGERED!

Endangered species in Judy's home state of Virginia:

- **northeast beach tiger beetle**
- **Shenandoah salamander**
- **monkeyface mussel**
- **shiny pigtoe**
- **bald eagle**

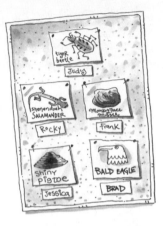

Find out about endangered species in your home state. Make a list here:

_____

_____

_____

_____

_____

_____

Find out three important fun facts about your
endangered species:

1. _____

2. _____

3. _____

Draw a picture of your endangered species:

Help Save the World!

Write about how you might try to save one of the endangered species in your state:

_____

_____

_____

_____

_____

_____

_____

_____

_____

_____

Endangered Species Word Match

Frank pointed to a beetle with a shiny green head and eyes like an alien. Printed below the beetle it said *Cicindela dorsalis dorsalis*.

"That's not a northeast beach tiger beetle," said Judy. "It's some kind of a Cinderella beetle."

"It's Latin," said Frank.

"Latin? Don't they have any beetles that speak English?"

Excerpt from *Judy Moody Saves the World!*

Can you match the scientific names of these endangered species to their common names? The first one is done for you. For the rest you might want to visit your library or look in some field guides! (Or check the answers at the back of the book.)

northeast beach tiger beetle	*Euphilotes battoides allyni*
El Segundo blue butterfly	*Fusconaia cor*
tooth cave spider	*Plethodon shenandoah*
shiny pigtoe	*Gambelia silus*
blunt-nosed leopard lizard	*Neoleptoneta myopica*
Shenandoah salamander	*Cicindela dorsalis dorsalis*

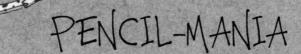

PENCIL-MANIA

Judy stopped chewing on her Grouchy pencil. She stared at it. The grouchy face looked even grouchier. This pencil used to be a tree. A rain forest tree!

She, Judy Moody, would never, ever use a pencil again.

Excerpt from *Judy Moody Saves the World!*

A few fun facts about pencils:

- ◉ One tree can make 172,000 pencils.

- ◉ One pencil can draw a line 35 miles long.

- ◉ One pencil can write 45,000 words!

- ◉ Benjamin Franklin advertised pencils for sale in his *Pennsylvania Gazette* in 1729.

- ◉ William Monroe, a cabinetmaker in Concord, Massachusetts, made the first American wood pencils in 1812.

- ◉ John Steinbeck wrote *The Grapes of Wrath* using as many as 60 cedar pencils every day!

- ◉ A pencil will write in zero gravity, upside down, and underwater!

- Seventy-five percent of the pencils sold in the United States are painted yellow! In the 1800s, this was to honor the Chinese and let people know that their pencils contained Chinese graphite — the best in the world!

- More than 2 billion pencils are used in the United States every year.

- Find out a fun fact about other school supplies. Check your library. Try an encyclopedia. Surf the Internet.

What can you find out about paper? Glue? Chalk? Erasers?

_____

_____

_____

_____

_____

_____

_____

Design Your Own T-Shirt!

Judy took out a fat marker and drew a
big-mouthed shark with lots of teeth.
I ATE A SHARK, she wrote in all capitals.

Excerpt from *Judy Moody*

Now it's your turn to design your own
T-shirt! Fill in Judy's blank shirt with
something YOU would like to wear on
the first day of school.

Design Your Own Band-Aid!

Judy Moody is crazy for Crazy Strips!

"Rare!" Judy said. "I, Judy Moody,
could have my own Crazy Strip."

Excerpt from *Judy Moody Saves the World!*

What design would YOU like to see on
knees, ankles, and elbows everywhere?

Doctor Judy Moody Jokes

What does a skeleton take for a cold?
Coffin drops!

What do skeletons put on their mashed potatoes?
Grave-y!

What do you call a skeleton who sleeps all day?
Lazybones!

What does a skeleton eat for breakfast?
Scream of wheat!

What did the doctor say to the patient with tonsillitis?
Have a swell *time!*

When did Benjamin Franklin discover electricity?
During a brain *storm.*

What's the hardest kind of bow to tie?
An elbow.

What do kidneys say at the start of a baseball game?
Bladder up!

How long can you hold your breath?
A lung, lung time.

Why did Toady go to the hospital?
To get a hop-er-a-tion.

If you breathe oxygen all day, what do you breathe at night?
Nightrogen!

What did the right eye say to the left eye?
Just between you and me, something smells.

What falls asleep but never snores?
Your foot.

Where does a sick boat go?
To the dock.

What do you call an operation on a rabbit?
A hare cut.

Bone Up on Your Bones!

Check out all the funny names for your bones!

face (cheekbone): zygoma
head: cranium
neck: cervical vertebrae
back: vertebral column
finger: phalange
arm: humerus
hip bones: ilium and ischium
leg (thigh): femur
knees: patellae
foot: metatarsus

Fill in the blanks with the funny-sounding names from George the Skeleton. (Answers at the back of the book.)

Pain in the __cervical vertebrae__

The bee's _____

Put your best _____ forward.

That's a _____ scratcher.

Red in the _____

Step on a crack, break your mother's _____

Costs a _____ and a _____

That's a _____ nail biter.

_____ , _____ , hooray!

Got a problem?
The doctor is IN.
Dr. Judy Moody,
that is!

Dear Judy,
I've got the hiccups!
How can I get rid of them?

Okay, which of the following is
NOT a cure for hiccups?
  a. standing on your head
  b. holding your breath
  c. eating a teaspoon of sugar
  d. blowing into a paper bag
  e. thinking of the color blue
  f. pinching your nose and
     drinking water
  g. jumping out of a plane
Tricked you! ALL of the above are
known cures for hiccups. No lie!

Dear Judy,
My mom bought me new
shoes for school and they
rub! What should I do if I
have a blister?

Blister? DON'T pop it. Instead,
think of words that rhyme with
blister: *mister, sister, kissed*
her *(yee-uk!)*.
See? Now, didn't that make you
forget about your blister?
No? Then go play Twister.

Dear Judy,
The lunch lady made me eat Brussels sprouts and now I feel sick. What should I do?

Okay, whatever you do, DON'T think of:
   a. worms
   b. slug slime
   c. ABC gum (Already Been Chewed)
   d. prunes
   e. toads
Better?
Oh well. I never said I was perfect.

Dear Judy,
Ow, I've got a headache!

When you have a plain, old-fashioned pain in your brain, you should ask your little brother to leave the room. You'll be amazed how fast your headache goes away! For sure and absolute positive! (If that doesn't work, try an ice pack.)

Dear Judy,
I have a frog in my throat! Any advice?

Absolutely.
You have three choices:
   a. Make it feel at home — swallow a tadpole.
   b. Open wide, say "ahh," and hope it hops out.
   c. Take two prunes and call your doctor in the morning.

The Phantom Doll Doctor Strikes Again

That's when Judy's brain began working on a brand-new Judy Moody idea.

She'd make a sign. Maybe set up shop in the garage. Get other kids to give her their broken dolls or old stuffed animals. Or she'd find some at yard sales. She would doctor them up and donate them to more sick kids in the Children's Wing at the hospital. Some could have Ace bandages, or fancy scars, or tubes for breathing. Maybe even an IV!

Excerpt from *Judy Moody Gets Famous!*

Help a sick kid in the hospital, just like Judy did! Here are some ideas to make kids feel better at a hospital near you:

- Write a letter to cheer somebody up.
- Make a get well card.
- Take them a teddy bear.
- Read a story.
- Make a cozy blanket to brighten up a hospital room.

Make a Fun and Fuzzy No-Sew Blanket! FOR REAL!

Make a cozy, warm blanket as a gift or for a needy kid. No sewing allowed!

1. At a fabric store, buy two different-colored pieces of polar fleece. The two pieces should be the same size, each slightly bigger than you want the final blanket to be. One handy size to try is a $1\frac{1}{2}$ x $1\frac{1}{2}$ yard square.

2. Spread one of the pieces of fleece flat on the floor, face-down. Lay the other piece directly on top of it, face-up, and line up the edges. You might want to pin the pieces together to keep them from shifting around. Trim any uneven edges.

3. Cutting through both layers with a pair of scissors, cut a 4-inch-by-4-inch square completely out of each corner.

4. Working your way around all four edges of the blanket, create a fringe with the scissors by making a 4-inch long cut every inch, again cutting through both layers of fleece.

5. Now it's time to join the top and bottom layers of fringe together. Starting at one corner, tie each 1-inch strip on the top layer to its matching strip on the bottom layer. Continue around the edges of the blanket until all the strips have been tied together. Remove any pins holding the layers together.

Voilà! Done!
It's that easy! No sewing!

Judy Moody Cootie Catcher

Moody? Broody? Or wriggly and giggly? Use the Judy Moody Cootie Catcher for some serious mood-acious advice!

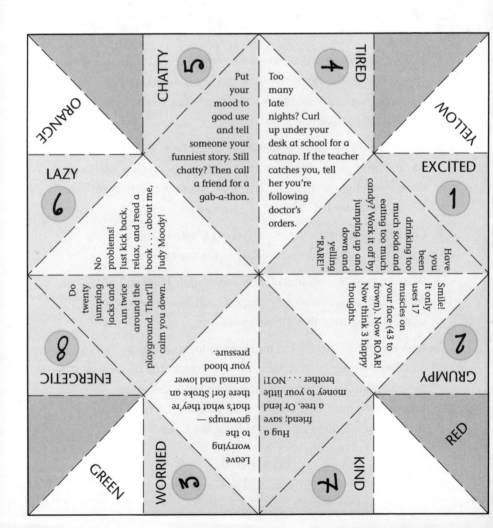

1. Photocopy and cut out the cootie catcher.

2. Printed side down, fold back all four corners to meet in the middle. Turn it over and do the same on the other side.

3. Fold it in half, with the color names facing out.

4. Now insert your thumbs and forefingers in the four square flaps, one in each flap, and hold them so they all meet at the center.

How to play:

1. Ask a friend to pick a color.

2. Spell out the color, opening the cootie catcher first one way, then the next for each letter.

3. Now get your friend to pick the word on the inside of the cootie catcher that best describes how he or she is feeling. Then count out the number beneath that word with the cootie catcher.

4. Ask your friend to choose a second word that best describes how he or she is feeling.

5. Now simply open the flap beneath that word for your Judy Moody mood advice!

Super Heroes and Heroines

Elizabeth Blackwell, First Woman Doctor

1821   Born in Bristol, England

1832   Comes to America

1847   After 28 rejections, is accepted to medical school

1849   Becomes first woman doctor, first in her class

1849   Moves to Paris, gets eye infection, loses vision in one eye

1853   Opens New York clinic for poor women and children

1854   Adopts Kitty Barry, a 7-year-old orphan from Ireland

1861   Trains nurses in the Civil War

1868   Opens first Women's Medical College

1876   Writes a book about children for parents

1910   Dies at the age of 89

Choose a person you admire.

Find out some facts about his or her life and make a timeline:

Year: **Important event:**

_____   _____

_____   _____

_____   _____

_____   _____

_____   _____

_____   _____

_____   _____

_____   _____

_____   _____

_____   _____

Elizabeth Blackwell

Lived in an attic
Nothing was automatic

First in her class
What more could you ask?

Became first woman doctor
Even though boys mocked her

Opened a clinic
Helped poor people in it

Delivered Babies
Gave shots for rabies (maybe)

Opened her own school
It was way cool

Wrote a book
Wonder how long it took

Born, I don't know when
Died, 1910

Take after the example
Of Dr. Elizabeth Blackwell

Excerpt from *Judy Moody, M.D.: The Doctor Is In!*

Write a poem about the person you most admire:

_____

_____

_____

_____

_____

_____

_____

_____

_____

_____

Judy Moody

Have you read all of the Judy Moody books?

Title: Judy Moody

Date Read:

Comments:

Title: Judy Moody Gets Famous!

Date Read:

Comments:

Title: Judy Moody Saves the World!

Date Read:

Comments:

Reading Checklist

 Title: Judy Moody Predicts the Future

Date Read:

Comments:

 Title: Judy Moody, M.D.: The Doctor Is In!

Date Read:

Comments:

What ideas do you have for more Judy Moody adventures?

What other good books have you been reading lately?

Megan McDonald's favorite book when she was a kid was *Harriet the Spy* by Louise Fitzhugh. Peter H. Reynolds's favorite book when he was a kid was *Charlie and the Chocolate Factory* by Roald Dahl. What are your favorite books? List them here:

 Title:

Date Read:

Comments:

 Title:

Date Read:

Comments:

 Title:

Date Read:

Comments:

Magic, Mysterious
Ever-Changing Mood Rings!

Mood rings change color with your mood!
Make up a mood for each color on your mood ring:

Blue: _____

Green: _____

Red: _____

Amber: _____

Purple: _____

Black: _____

If your mood ring had extra special magic powers, what would you wish for it to do?

Draw a picture of your ESP (Extra Special Powers) ring.

Does your magic ring have a name?

Magic 8 Ball

> "I know something that tells the future. You can ask a question and it's N-E-V-E-R wrong."
>
> Excerpt from *Judy Moody Predicts the Future*

Using the list of choices on the next page, what would you pick to answer each of these questions:

Will I get an A++ on my spelling test?

Will I eat a shark this summer?

Will I go to Disneyland?

Will I be president when I grow up?

Will I have a million dollars someday?

Will I dye my hair green?

Will I be a principal someday?

Will I write a book like *Judy Moody*?

* Signs point to yes.
* Yes.
* Reply hazy, try again.
* Without a doubt.
* My sources say no.
* As I see it, yes.
* You may rely on it.
* Concentrate and ask again.
* Outlook not so good.
* It is decidedly so.

* Better not tell you now.
* Very doubtful.
* Yes — definitely.
* It is certain.
* Cannot predict now.
* Most likely.
* Ask again later.
* My reply is no.
* Outlook good.
* Don't count on it.

Make up your own questions:

Will I _____ ?

Answer: _____

Will I _____ and live happily ever after?

Answer: _____

Will I ever _____?

Answer: _____

Will I _____ when I grow up?

Answer: _____

☀ Magic Potion ☀

Judy tries some magic spells and potions to find out if Mr. Todd is really in love.

Bowl of water + Apple Seed + Candle = true love

If you could make a magic potion, what would you want it to do?

Create your own recipe for a
magic potion here! Are there any
magic words that go along with
the potion?

_____

_____

_____

_____

_____

_____

_____

_____

Fun with Fortune Cookies!

May all your
moods be . . . R A R E!

You will get a big surprise
in the mail.

A new friend is in your future.

Uh-oh! A toad will pee on you.

Make up your own fortunes!

Judy Moody
Crossword Puzzle

Across

2. Judy found one in a cereal box.
3. Name of piano-playing chicken
7. Name of Judy's club with friends
13. Name of Judy's teacher
14. Northeast beach tiger _____
15. Name of Judy's cat
16. What Judy ate one summer

Down

1. State where Judy lives
4. Judy's saying when happy
5. Nickname for Stink
6. Name of Judy's Venus flytrap
8. Judy collects these
9. Name of Judy's tree
10. Kind of pencil Judy uses
11. Mouse knows how to make this.
12. _____ Blackwell, first woman doctor

(Answers at the back of the book.)

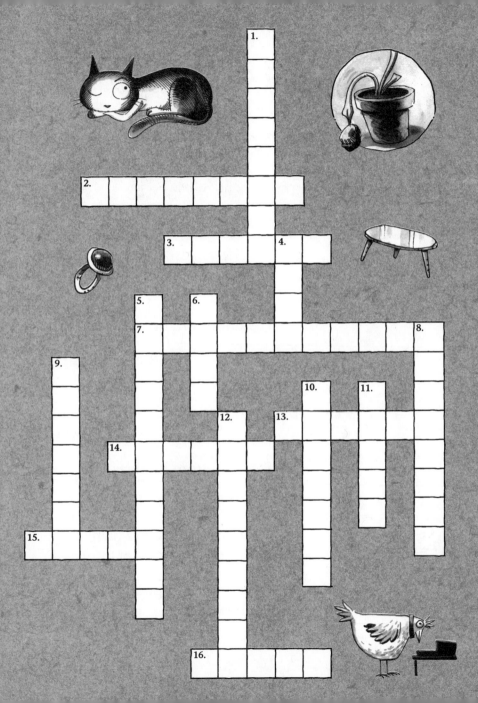

Judy Moody's Declaration of Independence

with 7 alien rights

I, Judy Moody, do hereby declare:

1. Freedom from brushing my hair

2. Freedom from little brothers (as in Stink)

3. Freedom from baby bedtime (as in staying up later than Stink)

4. Freedom from homework

5. Freedom to have sleepovers

6. Freedom to have my own bathroom (and washcloth!)

7. Freedom to get pounds of allowance

Excerpt from *Judy Moody Declares Independence*

Do you ever feel like you need more independence?
Judy Moody does! Here's your chance to create your own
Declaration of Independence — complete with alien rights.

_____ 's Declaration of

Independence with 7 alien rights

I, _____ , do hereby declare:

1.

2.

3.

4.

5.

6.

7.

The Law of the Sugar Packets

Sometimes, the best advice can be found in unusual places!

A penny saved is a penny earned.

Don't cry over spilled milk.

Fish and visitors stink after three days.

And sometimes, it's better just to write your own advice, like Judy does!

A penny saved is never as much as Stink has.

Don't cry over spilled chocolate milk.

Fish and little brothers stink after three days.

What words of advice would you
like to see on a sugar packet?
Start your own sugar packet collection!

Secret Code

Judy's parents sent Judy on a treasure hunt around their house using this secret code. This code was really used to send secret messages during the American Revolution!

A = Z		**J** = Q		**S** = H
B = Y		**K** = P		**T** = G
C = X		**L** = O		**U** = F
D = W		**M** = N		**V** = E
E = V		**N** = M		**W** = D
F = U		**O** = L		**X** = C
G = T		**P** = K		**Y** = B
H = S		**Q** = J		**Z** = A
I = R		**R** = I		

Can you decode these messages from Judy?

1. QFWB NLLWB IFOVH!

2. LMV RU YB OZMW, GDL RU YB HVZ

3. KILFW NVNYVI LU GSV GLZW KVV XOFY

4. ILZI!

(Answers at the back of the book.)

Now try creating your
own messages for
your friends!

_____

_____

_____

_____

_____

_____

_____

_____

Test Your Judy Moody I.Q.

Follow Your Star

WARNING: Even Judy Moody experts may be stumped! See how you rate in Judy Moody know-how. Check your answers at the back of the book.

Score (Number of correct answers)

1–6	**O**	**Oops!** Better read some more Judy Moody books!
7–12	**PG**	**Pretty Good.** Try sleeping with a Judy Moody book under your pillow.
13–18	**B**	**Brainiac.** You and Jessica Finch are Queen Bees.
19–24	**R**	**RARE!** You deserve a Thomas Jefferson tricorn-hat sticker.

Easy

1. What does the T. P. in T. P. Club stand for?

2. What did Frank Pearl eat for a dare?

3. What saying was on Judy's Crazy Strip when she entered the Band-Aid contest?

4. Name one thing Judy Moody likes to collect.

5. Who is the T. P. Club mascot?

6. What part of Judy got into the newspaper when she entered the pet contest?

7. What did Stink have to do to get into the T. P. Club?

8. What was written on the T-shirt that Judy wore the first day of school?

Medium

1. What is Mr. Todd's nickname?

2. What famous person does Judy most admire and want to grow up to be like?

3. What is Mouse's famous pet trick?

4. What does Stink feed to Judy's Venus flytrap?

5. What does Judy do to try to get 100% on her spelling test?

6. What did Stink's Crazy Strip say?

7. What subject is Jessica Finch especially good at in school?

8. When Mr. Todd put on Judy's mood ring, what color did it turn?

9. What does the color purple mean on the mood ring?

Difficult

1. What does Judy call Jessica Finch?

2. What ice-cream shop does Judy like to go to?

3. What kind of pencil does Judy like to write with?

4. What name do they print (by mistake) in the newspaper for Judy Moody?

5. Judy finds an old school project in the trash when she tries to get her family to recycle. What is it?

6. What shape is the stain on Judy's "Me collage" when Stink spills grape juice on it?

SUPERDUPER EXTRA-SPECIAL BONUS QUESTION:

What song did the chicken play on the piano at the pet show?

Looking to the Future . . .

The future was out there, waiting. And there was one more thing Judy did know for sure and absolute positive — there would be many more moods to come.

Excerpt from *Judy Moody Predicts the Future*

If you had one wish for the future, what would it be?

What's your biggest dream?

Make a list of five goals that you would like
to accomplish this year? Don't be afraid to
think big!

1.

2.

3.

4.

5.

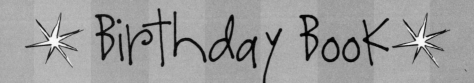

Birthday Book

Keep track of all of your
friends' birthdays here!

Name: **Birthday:**

Judy   April 1

Throw a birthday party with a Judy Moody theme!

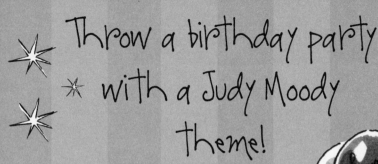

Here are some suggestions:

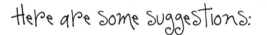

- ⊚ Decorate using the colors from the Judy Moody book covers (green and orange for example).

- ⊚ You may not have a Screamin' Mimi's near you, but you can still celebrate with ice cream! Get your favorite flavors and let everyone add their own toppings.

- ⊚ Have a fortune-telling area with a Magic 8 Ball!

- ⊚ Draw a big picture of Judy and play Stick-the-Band-Aid on Judy. Everyone wears blindfolds, and the person who sticks a Band-Aid closest to Judy's nose wins!

Print your name here:

Write your name in cursive here:

Doctors have messy autographs.
Sign your name like a doctor here:

Now sign it extra neatly:

Try writing with your left hand
(or right hand if you're a lefty!):

Want a real challenge? Try signing your name
with your foot here:

Get your friends to autograph your book here:

What famous person would you like to have
sign your book?

I like to be naughty.
I like to be nice.
But just to be moody
I'll sign my name twice.

Yours till Niagara Falls.
Yours till butter flies.
Yours till _____ wear roller skates.
Yours till _____ talk.
Yours till _____.

Roses are _____.
Violets are _____.
Give me _____ dollars.
And I will _____.

Igpay Atinlay

Jessica Finch likes to speak in Pig Latin.

Judy Moody = Udyjay Oodymay

Stink = Inkstay

Rocky = Ockyray

Frank = Ankfray

Jessica Finch = Essicajay Inchfay

Toady = Oadytay

Mouse = Ousemay

Jaws = Awsjay

Sign your name in Pig Latin:

Get your friends to sign their names in Pig Latin:

What is your pet's name in Pig Latin?

Which Judy Moody books have you read?

Judy Moody

Was in a moOd. Not a goOd mood. A bad mood.

Megan McDonald · Illustrated by Peter H. Reynolds

Judy Moody Gets Famous!

Megan McDonald · Illustrated by Peter H. Reynolds

Judy Moody Saves the World!

Megan McDonald · Illustrated by Peter H. Reynolds

Judy Moody Predicts the Future

Megan McDonald · Illustrated by Peter H. Reynolds

Judy Moody, M.D. The Doctor Is In!

Megan McDonald · Illustrated by Peter H. Reynolds

★ Judy Moody ★ Declares Independence

Megan McDonald · Illustrated by Peter H. Reynolds

Judy Moody Around the World in 8½ Days

Megan McDonald · Illustrated by Peter H. Reynolds

Judy Moody Goes to College

Megan McDonald · Illustrated by Peter H. Reynolds

Judy Moody & Stink THE HOLLY JOLIDAY

Megan McDonald · Illustrated by Peter H. Reynolds

Want to get acquainted with Judy in a hurry?

Try jump-starting your Judy Moody library
with these paperback collections.

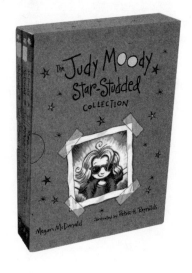

The Judy Moody Star-Studded Collection

What's better than one Judy Moody adventure? The first three Judy Moody adventures — in a single box. Rare!

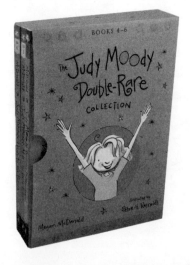

The Judy Moody Double-Rare Collection

Add to your Judy Moody collection with the fourth, fifth, and sixth adventures, boxed together for easy shelving!

The Judy Moody
Totally Awesome Collection
The first six Judy Moody adventures
in one instant collection. It's a
Moody-Palooza!

The Judy Moody Mood Journal
Feeling a little moody yourself? Check
out The Judy Moody Mood Journal.
This journal is perfect for writing
about what puts *you* in a mood! It's
also perfect for jotting down your
favorite knock-knock jokes, making a
Me collage, listing your favorite things,
writing down your dreams, and lots
more. So crack it open, sharpen your
Grouchy pencil, and get started!

Be sure to check out all of Stink's adventures!

Includes:
Stink: The Incredible Shrinking Kid
*Stink and the Incredible Super-Galatic
  Jawbreaker*
*Stink and the World's Worst Super-Stinky
  Sneakers*

Judy Moody has her own website!

Visit **www.judymoody.com**
for all things Judy Moody and lots
of way-not-boring stuff to do, including:

- ◉ All you need to know about the best-ever
  Judy Moody Fan Club

- ◉ Answers to all your V.I.Q.s (very important
  questions) about Judy

- ◉ Way-not-boring stuff about Megan McDonald
  and Peter H. Reynolds

- ◉ Double-cool activities that will be sure to put you
  in a mood—and not a bad mood, a good mood!

- ◉ Totally awesome T.P. Club info!

DOUBLE RARE!

Megan McDonald ———

is the best-selling author of all of the Judy Moody books, as well as the books about Judy's younger brother, Stink. "Sometimes I think I *am* Judy Moody," she says. "I'm certainly moody, like she is. Judy has a strong voice and always speaks up for herself. I like that." Megan McDonald and her husband live in Sebastopol, California. She is also the author of a middle-grade novel called *The Sisters Club*, a picture book called *Ant and Honey Bee*, illustrated by Brian Karas, and many other books for children.

Peter H. Reynolds ———

is the illustrator of all of the Judy Moody and Stink books. He recalls that when he was approached about illustrating *Judy Moody*, he jumped at the chance. The feisty, independent Judy reminded him of his own daughter, who was eleven years old at the time. Peter H. Reynolds lives in Dedham, Massachusetts. He is also the author-illustrator of several picture books, including *The Dot, Ish, So Few of Me,* and *The North Star*, as well as the illustrator of many other books for children.

ANSWERS

Antidisestablishmentarianism: The belief that the tie between church and state should not be removed

Hippopotomonstrosesquipedalian: Having to do with a very long word!

ENDANGERED SPECIES:

northeast beach tiger beetle
   Cicindela dorsalis dorsalis
El Segundo blue butterfly
   Euphilotes battoides allyni
tooth cave spider
   Neoleptoneta myopica
shiny pigtoe
   Fusconaia cor
blunt-nosed leopard lizard
   Gambelia silus
Shenandoah salamander
   Plethodon shenandoah

BONE UP ON YOUR BONES

cervical vertebrae (neck)
patellae (knees)
metatarsus (foot)
cranium (head)
zygoma (face)
vertebral column (back)
humerus, femur (arm, leg)
phalange (finger)
ilium, ischium (hip, hip)

CROSSWORD PUZZLE

ACROSS
2. mood ring
3. Mozart
7. Toad Pee Club
13. Mr. Todd
14. beetle
15. Mouse
16. shark

DOWN
1. Virginia
4. rare
5. Stinkerbell
6. Jaws
8. Band-Aids
9. Luna Two
10. Grouchy
11. toast
12. Elizabeth

SECRET CODE

1. Judy Moody rules!
2. One if by land, two if by sea
3. Proud member of the Toad Pee Club
4. ROAR!

QUIZ

(Easy)

1. Toad Pee
2. paste
3. Heal the World
4. Band-Aids, scabs, pizza tables, spare doll parts
5. Toady
6. her elbow
7. have a toad pee on him
8. I ATE A SHARK

(Medium)

1. Mr. Toad
2. Elizabeth Blackwell
3. making toast
4. raw hamburger
5. sleep with the dictionary under her pillow
6. Batty for Band-Aids
7. spelling
8. red
9. Joyful, on top of the world

(Difficult)

1. Queen Bee or Jessica (Flunk) Finch or Jessica *Aardwolf* Finch or Jessica Fink
2. Screamin' Mimi's
3. Grouchy
4. Judy Muddy
5. her Laura Ingalls Wilder log cabin
6. Virginia

(Superduper Extra-Special Bonus Question)

"Three Blind Mice"